# Mirror of the Prodigal Son
## The Power of Reconciliation
### Volume 2

Akili Xzavier Williams

*2nd Chance Publishing*

# Endorsements/Reviews

Mirror of the Prodigal Son: The Power of Reconciliation has been constructed to help those who have found themselves in a vagabonded state, come to the realization that though we aren't worthy, his grace is sufficient enough to restore us back to our place of sonship in the Kingdom. This book will call you to a place of repentance and back into the loving arms of our Heavenly Father.

**Larry Baker**
**Pastor of United For Christ Ministries**

In "Mirror of The Prodigal Son", Dr. Akili Williams has combined wisdom, practical truth and tons of encouragement. The message in "The Mirror of the Prodigal Son" is tremendous and prompted by the very heart of God. This book has the power to change the lives of specific Fathers, sons, family relations of those who are willing to do the necessary work of adhering to the principles outlined in it. Dr. Akili Williams discusses the need for a radical shift in consciousness; in the way we think and the development stages of sons in cultivating balanced relations, our potential and possibilities. Mirror of The Prodigal Son' can be read through in a single setting, however, the timeless, principles in its pages should be meditated upon daily. This book is highly recommended and should be used as a text book for churches, and other organizations committed to developing tomorrow's leaders and restoring the divine order of sonship and the rights toward their inheritance.

**Dr. Israel Prince Barsh, D.DiV**
**Sr. Prophet/Pastor, Dominion International**
**Spiritual Truth Embassy**

Dr. Akili Williams has written a heartfelt account of his faith journey where "warts and all" he tells his story of being the prodigal son and his return to the Father. This book is highly recommended for the lost and the found alike.

**Gary Lee Frye, Ed.D., GPC**
**Homeless Liaison / Grant Writer**
**Lubbock-Cooper ISD**

It is with the utmost thanks and appreciation that I give God praise for you, your experiences of life and the grace of God he bestowed upon you through reconciliation. When we come to realize that we are inadequate to run this Christian Journey alone, it is then we need to ask God's help. God is a God of a second chance. It is vitally important that we stay focus on Christ and not lose eye and heart contact with him.

God is a God of Reconciliation for everyone that believes. Yours in Christ, God Moma

**Dr. Lennie O. Gaskins, Sr. Pastor**
**Praise Temple, F.B.C.**

First and foremost I would like to say congratulations to my husband (Dr. Akili Xzavier Williams, you have made a huge accomplishment and not only am I proud of you, I know Devin and Akilah are as well! In reading your book, I felt it to be very easy and understandable. Also, I could follow its meaning as I know other readers will. This book not only captures a central theme, but also draws comparisons and solutions, with the central theme as a guideline. Akili states the obvious, with personal experience and conviction. Akili has proven that when you're willing to accept Jesus Christ in your life, you can have it all.

**Amy Romain-Williams**
**Inside Out Transition Consults, Inc**
**Ft. Lauderdale, Florida**

# Special Thanks/Acknowledgements

First, I give all glory, praise, and honor to God, the maker of all. I thank him for giving me both the opportunity and the ministry of reconciliation.

I thank God for my lovely wife. She stimulates a drive in me, which is unmatched. I'm grateful for her love and support. I'm also thankful for my fantastic children. They inspire me tremendously and motivate me by their faith in me. I want to thank my mother and father for their support and diligence in dealing with me. Love you all.

To all of the members and partners of New Direction Bible Fellowship, I say thank you. Thank you for putting your faith in me as your Apostolic Voice and Father. Thank you all.

Thank you, Apostle Dennis & Angela Maxwell, for imparting wisdom and knowledge. Thank you for pushing and motivating me to obtain Destiny. Thank you, for birthing and mentoring me in the deliverance ministry. Thank you both.

Thank you, Dr. Israel Prince, for activating and birthing the prophetic in my life. Thank you, for mentoring me in business, ministry, and the prophetic. Thank You Prophet.

Thank you, Pastor Larry Baker, you have proven to be a friend among friends. Thank you, for having the heart of God. Thank you Apostle

Thank you, Pastor Torrey Phillips, you are a tremendous gift to me, I'm grateful for our friendship. For being an Apostolic Voice and a mentor.
Thank you, Doc

Thank you, John Longobardi, you are a great friend. Thank you for believing in me and sticking by me.
Thank you, Big Dawg

# Dedication

To my best friend and companion, my lovely wife Amy Romain-Williams, for motivating and pushing me, to become who God has ordained me to be. To my children Devin James and Akilah D'yana, your belief in me has created volumes of Aspirations and Inspiration. To my deceased grandparents C.D. & Emma Derico, for giving me a solid, Christian foundation and assuring me that Gods love was never ending. This book is dedicated to you.

*AKILI XZAVIER WILLIAMS*

# Table of Contents

# Foreword

Love and forgiveness are the very soul of the gospel
message. Man has a profound sense of estrangement, of being lost, and ultimately, whether aware of it or not, this lostness stems from separation from God. As the ancient writer prayed, "Thou hast made us for thyself, and our heart is restless until it rests in thee.

Paul writes:
*18"All this is from God, who reconciled us to himself through Christ and gave us the ministry of reconciliation: 19that God was reconciling the world to himself in Christ, not counting men's sins against them. And he has committed to us the message of reconciliation. 20We are therefore Christ's ambassadors, as though God were making his appeal through us. We implore you on Christ's behalf: Be reconciled to God. 21God made him who had no sin to be sin for us, so that in him we might become the righteousness of God. (2 Corinthians5:18-21)*

The key concept here is "reconciliation." The idea here is restoring a relationship between two parties. Author John Stott calls reconciliation "the opposite of alienation." In the New Testament, God is the offended party to whom man must be reconciled, a feat achieved through the redemptive work of the cross.

In *The Mirror of the Prodigal Son*, Dr. Akili Williams exposes the deepest need of humanity, Reconciliation. As he shares from his personal experiences and God given wisdom, we have the opportunity to glean from his life without enduring the pain of his process, what a marvelous contribution Dr. Akili Williams leaves on record for years to come. We are better because of his unselfishness. Read this book with the expectation of being challenged and changed forever.

**Torrey Phillips, Pastor/Author**
**Impact Word Church**
**Pompano Beach, Florida**

# Introduction

I am so excited to share this book with you. Firstly, I want you to understand that, like many of you, I would consider myself the prodigal son. This book provides the story why I make this statement by giving you a parallel account of both the Prodigal Son's life and mine. I know that so many of you come from turbulent pasts. While some of you are struggling with identity and a place to belong, others are backsliding and lost their relationship with the Father. I pray that after you read this book, everything that is holding you captive from your past, releases you. I pray that you find yourself in the arms of the Father and that you take your rightful place as a son or daughter. I pray that you find your way back home in the service of the Father.

Secondly, I want you to know that it's taken me, what seems like ages to return to my rightful place. From the time that I backslid and reconciled back to God was a stretch of 12 years. Wow, that's a long time. I am so grateful to God for his mercy and his grace. Without the two, I would not be here now. It has been a long tedious journey. I have been through a lot of struggles and hardships. But I can honestly say, I wouldn't give anything for my journey.

Thirdly, I want you to seriously evaluate your present life. Think about where you are right now. Also, take a mental journey into the past; consider everything that has transpired and the outcomes. Compare the two; make a mental note of where you were spiritually, through those times. I am sure like myself you will find that you were away from God. It is my endeavor, to bring you back to God, bring you back to a place of safety, a place of love, and a place of peace.

Wow, this is so exciting for me, to be able to share The Power of Reconciliation with you. It is both a joy and pleasure. I have made the ministry of Reconciliation a primary goal of mines. Bringing mankind back to God one person at a time is the mandate of my ministry. The bible says in 2 Corinthians 5:18 "All this is from God, who reconciled us to Himself through Christ and gave us the ministry of reconciliation": So after reconciling me back to Him through Christ, He has given me the ministry of reconciliation. Which is to bring you back to him, Isn't that just wonderful, how the strategy of God is. After reading Mirror of the Prodigal Son, I pray that you turn every area of your life back to God and share this message of Reconciliation, so that others can do the same. Thank you for giving me this opportunity to share this message with you.

**Dr. Akili Xzavier Williams**

# CHAPTER ONE
## I Can Take Care of Myself

*"The finest inheritance you can give to a child is to allow it to make its own way, completely on its own feet"*
*-Isadora Duncan*

*"My country owes me nothing. It gave me, as it gives every boy and girl, a chance. It gave me schooling, independence of action, opportunity for service and honor. In no other land could a boy from a country village, without inheritance or influential"*
*-Herbert Hoover*

All of us started out with the potential of Greatness. Initially we were given everything we needed to succeed, survive, and prosper. In the book of Genesis, the bible paints a vivid picture of the Garden of Eden. There was a river that went through the garden for water. This river was so big it was split into four canals. The largest having gold, bdellium, and onyx stones, it was a rich river. There were trees that bore fruit and plants that bore fruits and vegetables. God even gave man privilege to eat of every tree and plant in the garden except one. Being a child of God is awesome, because quite naturally everything that is his is ours.(Psalms 25:13 "He will spend his days in prosperity, and his descendants will inherit the land.") (Psalms 16:5 "LORD, you

have assigned me my portion and my cup; you have made my lot secure"). We are granted an inheritance from God the moment that we accept Him as Lord and Savior of our lives. This inheritance doesn't only include riches (material wealth), but spiritual wealth as well. As a part of my personal testimony, I was saved at the early age of 7 years old and preached my first sermon at the age of 9 years old. I was granted everything my little heart desired. I would do revivals everywhere and people would bless me tremendously.

Eventually I like the Prodigal Son and many of us; I was overtaken by self will. Sometimes we tend to lose focus of the big picture so to speak. The picture that God is forever playing before our eyes, but it's that picture that we close our eyes to.

We forget that God, our Father has saved us to render service unto Him. Yes the big picture is, He grants us everything we could ever ask or think, so that we can worship and work for Him. This is why Jesus says that we have to deny ourselves if we desire to serve Him (Luke 9:23 "LORD, you have assigned me my portion and my cup; you have made my lot secure"). Judas paid for acting out of self-will, with his life and wasn't given the chance of reconciliation. (Matthew 26:14-16 Then one of the Twelve--the one called Judas Iscariot--went to the chief priests 15 and asked, "What are you willing to give me if I hand him over to you?" So they counted out for him thirty silver coins. 16 From then on Judas watched for an opportunity to hand him over).

This is why the parable of the Prodigal Son is so important, so that we understand the steps we must take to find ourselves back into the service of the Father. The first step to reconciliation is accepting the will of God for our lives. This son decided that he wanted to do what he wanted to do. He wanted to get up when he wanted to. He wanted to party when he felt the urge to party. He wanted to eat what he wanted to eat. He wanted to hang out with who he wanted to hang out with. I can mirror all the actions of the Prodigal Son, because like the youngest son in the parable self-will got in the way of my relationship with the Father. Funny thing about self-will the Father gave it to us. He gives us the choice to do His will or ours, of course there is a penalty for putting our will as his, but we do have the choice.

This son asked his father to give him his portion of the inheritance, so he could pleasure his will and not his fathers. Later in this book you will see where self-will got him. I recall times where I would leave a revival and go to the club. I had gotten so caught up in the things the self wanted, that the things of God were obsolete in my mind. Eventually like the Prodigal Son I wanted the riches without the services. I wanted the cake and the ice cream at the same time. Weird thing is for awhile I thought I was actually having them both. As I stated before I would preach, lay hands, prophesy, and give words of knowledge then go be subject to my own will. For a while I had one foot in and one foot out or what the old folks used to call straddling the fence. I was notorious for wearing the strap on clergy collar. As soon as I was done with service, it was time to snatch the collar off and go find the party. Talk about straddling the fence. It wasn't long till my will had become superior and it just didn't matter, so I resigned from ministry and service of The Father.

There was another trait that played a part in me taking my portion of goods and wandering off to a far country. That trait is selfishness. When self-will and selfishness team up, destruction is on the way. The two together will paint a picture of the mundane elements of this world, a picture that looks very inviting. And no matter what dilemma you are in you will be tempted to join the party. It didn't matter who saw me or who knew, it just seemed the grass was greener on the other side. Oh yes, being blessed with everything I wanted caused me to want more and more. I would be blessed with 2 suits then I'd want two more. I would be blessed with a new robe and I would want 1 more. It got to the point that I was only concerned with self. These acts of selfishness and others caused me to fall from the will of God. Looking back at all of the pain and suffering, I realize that it was no one but the love of God that kept me. (Hebrews 12:6 "For whom the Lord loves he chastens, and scourges every son whom he receives").

I remember thinking Akili what is your problem, God has given you everything that you could ever want or imagine. He has deeded you everything that you need, all for your willful service. But because of selfishness, I caused myself to undergo years of spankings. Selfishness will cause us to lose focus of God's will for our life. The Prodigal Son had everything and all he had to do was be about his father's business, to take advantage of it all. All he had to do was supervise workers in the field, the occasional chore here or there. Assist in cultivating, planting, and the harvest. He had a beautiful and desirable life. Many would have given all to have been in the Prodigal sons shoes. However, this son was not satisfied, he wanted more than what he had. Acting out of selfishness, the Prodigal Son, desired to make his own rules and hours of employment.

Not considering how his father had previously provided for him, he figured he was big enough to take care of himself, with his father's riches of course. This son had grown so selfish, that he didn't care how his father's affairs would be handled, he wanted to enjoy himself. I'm reminded of the joy I would have when someone would accept Christ as their savior and would be healed, during a revival. While doing mission work, I'd be overwhelmed with happiness that little ole' me could be used of God to assist another. I'm also reminded of how selfish I was to stop allowing God to use me for his glory. In contrast the two memories make me appreciate where I am presently and the experience of God's grace.

Like the story of the Prodigal Son, after the father had taken him back and allowed him to come back home; so did God, my father took me back. Sometimes I wonder what if the prodigal's father would not have been a forgiven and tolerate father. Even while knowing that his son was not responsible enough to handle himself, he still allowed him the opportunity to experience the other side of life. Now we notice the son taking a journey into a far country. This is where the separation or backsliding happens. In my life I didn't have to go far to be in a far country. When you find yourself more concerned about your will rather than God's will that's the far country. When it's not first or second nature for you to praise and pray you are in the far country. It was in the far country that I was allowed to use the portion of goods that I was given.

The far country experience initially is cool. In the beginning I was so overwhelmed, with my new found freedom, that I felt I was in the right place. The thing about being separated from God is, we separate from him, and he doesn't separate from us. The bible tells us that God is married to the backslider (Jeremiah 3:14 "Return, faithless people," declares the LORD, "for I am your husband). So even in while we are in the far country squandering our inheritance, he still stands with his arms stretched wide. See we are saved by grace, not by works, so just because we turn our backs on him, he doesn't turn his grace from us. Grace is unmerited, so there is nothing you can do to earn it.

Apostle Paul says his grace is sufficient for us (2 Corinthians12:9 But he said to me, "My grace is sufficient for you, for my power is made perfect in weakness." Therefore I will boast all the more gladly about my weaknesses, so that Christ's power may rest on me). It's in the separation period that we began to lose the traits of Godliness. While some traits may be noticeable others will die. In my separation, I was still able to give words of knowledge and prophesy, but I couldn't love or have peace. I can imagine the Prodigal Son, having the mind to prosper but couldn't effectively make business decisions. Everyone he met knew he was different, but he wasn't living the part.

While separated from the father we seek the former traits of Godliness, but not in the arms of the father. This is called the sensualization period. We seek love, joy, happiness, and peace etc., everywhere except in the arms of the father. We get so caught up in finding what we used to have, while we were in the arms of the father, that we begin to spite our father's will and in many cases even his existence. In the far country the things that once gave us joy begin to no longer give us joy. And because we aren't in tune with Gods will any longer, we allow the natural man to take control. So our natural senses take over, we act out of sensualization.

Many marriages are broken, in the far country. Spouses lose the focus of their vows and try to fill the void with extra marital affairs. Careers are shattered in the far country. Late night escapades and midnight marauders cause us to be unproductive and eventually lose employment. No longer having a relationship with the father, causes mental anxieties, feeding the carnal man with any and everything it desires. Anxiety eventually causes depression, mental illnesses, and physical illnesses. During this time our prayer life, Christian fellowship, and belief is dead.

# CHAPTER TWO
### Losing It All

*"What the horrors of war are, no one can imagine.
They are not wounds and blood and fever, spotted
and low, or dysentery, chronic and acute, cold and
heat and famine. They are intoxication, drunken
brutality, demoralization and disorder on the part of
the inferior... jealousies, meanness, indifference,
selfish brutality on the part of the superior."
-Florence Nightingale*

*"Are you upset little friend? Have you been lying
awake worrying? Well, don't worry...I'm here. The
flood waters will recede, the famine will end, the sun
will shine tomorrow, and I will always be here to take
care of you".
-Charlie Brown*

In many cases, while in the far country, we allow
our fleshly desires to get obese. I remember my
travels through the far country. I no longer would
fellowship with God or the church. There was no
more shame about anything. I didn't care who saw me
drinking, smoking, clubbing, or partying. I no longer
had the urge to hide. This is when Spiritual

Destitution arrives. The institution of holiness was gone. Once we get so far gone in the far country, we become adapted to its protocols. While once being led and guiding by the Holy Spirit, now we are led and guided by our own sinful nature. The scripture describes this as a reprobate mind (Romans 1:28 And, even as they did not like to retain God in their knowledge, God gave them over to a reprobate mind, to do those things which are not convenient.) It's where your new found regimes become the norm. The regime you had in prior times are abnormal. In the first stage factors of the far country, we feel we have to hide or we feel uneasiness in our newly found citizenship.

Now while spiritual destitution sets in the feeling is vice versa. If we were to visit the church or make contact with former friends or brethren, we feel we have to hide from our new clique. At this point we find every excuse in the world not to engage with anyone or thing that has to do with our former relationship with father. I recall during my stage of spiritual destitution, I physically relocated myself, so that the chances of contact with the brethren were virtually impossible. I found myself never praying, studying the bible, or fellowshipping. Instead, I spent all my time partying, getting high, and indulging in habits of the flesh. For many of us this happens so fast, we never realize how we made it there. Jesus told Peter that Satan wanted to sift him like wheat. Likewise with us the devil is allowed to tempt us so, that he vividly supplies everything our flesh desires. We have all heard the saying "Much Prayer, Much Power". In retrospect the same is vice versa, "No Prayer, No Power".

When we get so engulfed in feeding our flesh, our spirit becomes lack. And once your spirit gets weak, we give in more & more to fleshly desires. Now the sifting grinds your spirit finer & finer, until we're spiritually destitute. In the story of the Prodigal Son, he had spent all that he had. He became destitute of all the moral fiber, financial sustenance, and self-awareness that he had gotten from his father. Notice that it wasn't until he had lost it all, that the famine came. It wasn't until he had no more to put out that there was no more to get. Subsequently, it was when there was no more to get, that the son had become in need. Now, this son is in want; found himself discontent and impoverished.

Life was a revolving door of sin and shame. In our lives we find that no matter what we did to improve our wellbeing, didn't work. There is a constant arousal of the flesh and nothing to tantalize our spirit man. Because of our surroundings, we only succumb to the needs of the flesh. The spiritual connection is lost, so nothing links us to growth. I recall the mind frame I had in this stage. The thought of abandonment was ever present. I blamed everyone but myself for my state of being. All hope of who I knew I was predestined to be, was gone. The chain of fellowship with the father was broken. Because there was no spiritual insight, I was blinded by the darkness. I couldn't see where I was and certainly couldn't envision, where I had to go.

Now while spiritually hopeless, I like the Prodigal Son had to start to relinquish that lofty and proud mindset that I had taken when first arriving in the far country. This state of being is called self abasement. While not yet ready to return to the father, the

Prodigal Son made himself as citizen of the far country. This part of the story hits home with me, for this is exactly what I did. Imagine this, preacher turned drug dealing, drug addict, now becoming a disc jockey, and club promoter, doing a total 360 degree change. That brings the saying "if you can't beat them join them" to life. This was the perfect way to live the life I wanted to live (drugging, partying, and whoring) and make money doing it. However, at the same time I was bringing myself lower and lower.

Like the Prodigal Son, this was the scenario of feeding the swine. Little did I know that my drug addiction would reach a height that would be unbearable? Little did I know that the wear and tear to on my body from partying would almost kill me? Little did I know that the sexual promiscuity would nearly destroy my relationship with my baby's mama (present day wife)? The whole act of becoming a citizen of the far country was me allowing myself to stoop down and become the very thing that I was against and said I would never become. Look in the mirror yourself and consider when God had to bring you down in order to pick you up. Like the Prodigal Son, we thought becoming a citizen, would sustain us, but little did we know God has a plan to bring us back to him. It's like climbing a ladder you can only go so high before you have to come down only to go up again.

It's not until you come down that you realize that you need a constant relationship with the father to culminate and maintain. I remember thinking, wow, how did I go from having it all, to having nothing. In the self-abasement stage, that's exactly what happens. A certain consciousness is born. You can visualize where you are and where you've come from. However, because you still haven't undergone the total recourse of leaving the fathers safety, you wallow in your filth, shame, and sin. I vividly recall, losing my children and their mother (present day wife). Losing the only somewhat stability that I had, my family. For some of us it doesn't take to be brought down this low, but for others like me, this is when you begin to feel the lowest of the low.

It's in the self-abasement stage that, mental illnesses take course and self-worthlessness becomes a friend. Depression moves in next door. Anxiety is a salesman that pops up from time to time. It's hard to be productive when you physically and mentally don't have any motivation, when you mentally beat yourself up so much until your body acts out the pain. I remember when my body began to get sick. My lymph nodes began to swell. After going to the doctor and having cultures taken. I was told that I possibly had lymphoma. Already in the depressed mental state I was in, I figured I was done so let me give life a hand. I went to a mainstream electronic dance show and took loads of drugs, to induce an overdose. To no avail the ecstasy, meth, acid, ketamine, and cocaine didn't do its intended job. I remember hanging out and thinking, no one knows this is my last show, that this is it for me. I was hoping to just end it all, but it obviously wasn't my time. God had other plans for my life as does he for your life. A week later I found out that it wasn't cancer, it was just an infection.

God knows how to get our attention, doesn't he? Many of us have been brought down so low that either we had to dig in and find a little hope to trust God or just give up. Self-abasement is a vital stage of reconciliation. When you get all the way down, that's when you can look up.

# CHAPTER THREE
## Dirty Work

*"The most solid comfort one can fall back upon is the thought that the business of one's life is to help in some small way to reduce the sum of ignorance, degradation and misery on the face of this beautiful earth."*
*- George Eliot*

*"The world is more than the sum of its suffering".*
*-Deepak Chopra*

As we look deeper & clearer into the mirror. We see a sinful state, a lifestyle in enmity with God. We see perpetual dissatisfaction; this son had completely lost it. The prodigal son had arrived at the lowest point on the totem pole that one can be. While low and in want the Prodigal Son, put himself in service. He went to the labor pool, only to find a menial of occupations. Not service of the house; which he would be content & rather familiar, but the field, feeding the swine. Not just a menial job, but a job that was poor in sustenance as well. So low and so hungry he happily filled his belly and satisfied his hunger and nourished his body with the hurls, or something he wouldn't normally eat. Like many of us, in this stage: we try to fill the void, with prescription medication: some try to fill it with sexual promiscuity.

We absorb so much garbage in our spirit, souls, and bodies; and still aren't sustained. The same stuff that caused us to depart from our father and once gave us satisfaction now disappoints us; we are working in vain. The book of Isaiah asked a question to us that are in this stage (Isaiah 55:2-"Why do you spend money for what is not bread, and your wages for what does not satisfy"?). The same sin that once brought us joy and sustenance will no longer bring joy or sustenance. All that we once indulged in and filled our total man now fills nothing. The little bit that we do make feeding the swine, will never amount to what we had while with the father.

This over lapse of void is part of God's wrath or chastisement. As (Hebrew 12:6 states "for those whom the lord loves he disciplines, and he scourges every son whom he receives"). So when you make it to this stage, you're a just a little bit closer to being reconciled to the father. In this stage you are starving and are in need of sustainability: not just physically, but spiritually. It will be hard to continue, if you don't get sustenance soon. However nothing that you do seems to fill the void within you. Take note of Ezekiel 7:19-"They will fling their silver into the streets and their gold will become an abhorrent thing ;

their silver and their gold will not be able to deliver them in the day of the wrath of the LORD. They cannot satisfy their appetite nor can they fill their stomachs, for their iniquity has become an occasion of stumbling". God allows us to starve, so that we understand that without him we have nothing.

That we are only stewards and it is our job to live for him and handle his affairs. The Prodigal Son tried to earn food by working, he relied on begging: however no one gave him anything, because they knew his suffering was self-inflicted. This young man's appearance was feeble & skinny; and he provoked people, because he felt they owed him the favor. He had partied with them, had loaned them money, and had parlayed with them. However, now no one will help him, no man will assist him in his need. This shows that when we depart from God, that no one or nothing can help us, but him. The world and its gods, which we have served, gave us all which poisoned our soul, but has nothing to give that will nourish it. I remember when I got hungry and began searching in places (spiritually) that I couldn't find any nourishment that sustained me. I remember thinking of Jesus' words in (John 6:35-Jesus said to them, "I am the bread of life; he who comes to me will not hunger, and he who believes in me will never thirst").

It was then that I stopped looking in those places, because they would never be able to feed me. Many of us are still looking in the dry void place. Let me ask you a question, how can a void dry place sustain a void dry place? Answer, they can't, the only place that you will be sustained, is back in the arms of the

father.

# CHAPTER FOUR
## Lord Help Me

*"Other than us staying here for a while, I don't even see myself as a victim because there are people who have lost family members, have lost everything they worked for in life and don't know when they're going to get their next meal or their next bottle of water. It's easy for me to stay focused knowing that those people are the ones who are struggling and not me. I've been blessed enough to be able to get out of there and get some of my things out of there."*
*-Donte' Stallworth*

*"Life is perpetually creative because it contains in itself that surplus which ever overflows the boundaries of the immediate time and space, restlessly pursuing its adventure of expression in the varied forms of self-realization."*
*-Rabindranath Tagore*

While in all this madness and frenzy, Gods arms are yet open. Even though we turned our backs on him; he never turns his back on us. It's up to us to realize his mercy and grace. Let's take a look at the Prodigal Son's mental state while in the far country. The bible says he came to himself, this intimates that all this time he had not been himself. I remember while I was out there, in the far country, I would hear people whisper Akili doesn't seem like himself. The truth of the matter is I wasn't myself. I'm sure the prodigal was himself when he first left his father's house. When he first arrived in the far country he still had some of the same persuasions that he had at his father's house.

However, as time progressed, those persuasions began to change. Once this son got entangled with all the lust of the flesh, it made him crazy. In the midst of craziness he came to himself. It took for him to be in want, to come to the state of realization. Many of us like the Prodigal Son are either case; there are 4 factors we must take into consideration concerning the realization stage. (1) The situation that caused him to realize. It was his starving; when he was in want, then he came to himself. Consider that God in his infinite wisdom & grace strategically sets & sanctified, situations that leads us back to him. When we have searched everywhere with no avail of comfort, we must turn back to him. Now, with these new found experiences of error, we will become eager to do what it takes to be back in the arms of safety. (2) The act of consideration, he said within himself. Once he came back to his normal mind frame, he reflected on his present situation and his past situation.

[1] He considered what his present situation was. His present situation was not only bad but terrible, and he was perishing. He expected no relief at this point; he stated that he was perishing with hunger. Many times in our lives, while in this state; we feel embarrassed to turn back to the father. However, this state is the one that forces us back into his arms. He is still standing there with open arms, waiting for you to return and honored to take us back.

[2] He considered his former condition, while with his father. He thought about all the servants that worked for his father, how they had bread to spare. He began to reminisce on all the good times that he had, enjoying life with his family. He had flash backs

of the times that he upset his father, but was still given everything he needed. What more for us to consider a father that has everything? Consider what (Psalms 24:1 says about God's riches, "The earth is the Lord's and all that is in it, the world, and those who live in it").

This consideration played a vital role in my own reconciliation to the father. After I was sick and tired of being sick and tired. It's was when I was sick of struggling and losing out on everything, that I considered my father. I thought about how good everything was, while I was with my father. I thought about how even during suffering, the father always prepared a table before me. (3) How could he fix what he had broken (the relationship with the father). He took in consideration of all that he had been through and came to a conclusion: I will arise, and go to my father.

The Prodigal Son realized he had messed up and his intent was honest. He knew his father was loving and tenderhearted, from prior experiences. He knew his father would forgive him. [1] He figured out what to do: I will arise, and go to my father. After all the contemplating, he decided not to waste anymore time, but will arise and go. Even though he was far away, he would use the same determination he used to leave, to get back home. Many times we feel that because we have made the decision to go back to the father, that we should be given some extra strength or help. But every step we take after leaving fellowship with the father should be a step back to him. It's funny how it seems it takes more time to get back to the father, than it did when we left. However, once we understand the power of reconciliation, we make this process more expedient. Personally once I understood reconciliation, it didn't take long before I was back in the arms of the father. [2] He figured out what to say. This point is pivotal, because what we say to the father in repentance must be deliberate. Like the Prodigal Son we must be true to ourselves as well as the father and spill our guts so to speak.

First, the prodigal confessed his defective behavior and his foolish actions. He confessed: I have sinned. Admitting that everything he had done was wrong. He took ownership of his actions. The bible says in (Romans 3:23, that all have sinned and come short of the glory of God). So no one is exempt from being a sinner. But to truly be reconciled, we must take ownership of our sins. Secondly, he showed overall guilt for his sins: I have sinned against heaven, and before thee. We must show guilty concern for all we have done while in the far country. True reconciliation causes us to make amends for the things we have done. I've found that my relationship with the father gets stronger every time I right a past wrong; try it.

Thirdly, he executed judgment upon himself. Notice he says I am no longer worthy to be called thy son. The fact that he was indeed his son was the one thing the Prodigal Son could hold to. However, at this point he knew that there was the chance that the father could deny his son ship. So he readily showed contrition and condemned himself. I remember when I rededicated my life to the father. I had this awareness that I wasn't worthy of the love and forgiveness I had received. I remember making a pact with myself. This pact declared my gratitude, I declared that I would serve him in so, that I would try to make up for the time I was in the far country. The process of realization allows us to evaluate where we were, where we are, and where we want to be.

*AKILI XZAVIER WILLIAMS*

# CHAPTER FIVE
## Take Me Back

*"Always bear in mind that your own resolution to succeed is more important than any one thing."*
*-Abraham Lincoln*

*"Thus conscience does make cowards of us all; and thus the native hue of resolution is sick lied o'er with the pale cast of thought, and enterprises of great pith and moment with this regard their currents turn awry, and lose the name of action"*
*-William Shakespeare*

In the preceding chapter we dealt with realization, opening our eyes to whom we are and where we are. In this chapter we will deal with the three critical (R) actions in the process of reconciliation. (1) Resolution, figuring out a solution to make things right with the father. (2) Repentance, turning back in the direction of the father. (3) Return back into the loving arms of the father. Let's note that the prodigal rationalized his resolve. He came to terms and grips, the very reality that he had messed up and needed to fix what he had messed up. Some people actually don't believe that they have wronged anyone. While others, will never admit to wronging anyone. Either way it is important for us to realize on a daily basis, our current state.

As, Jesus taught, he said [23] "Therefore, if you are offering your gift at the altar and there remember that your brother or sister has something against you, [24] leave your gift there in front of the altar. First go and be reconciled to them; then come and offer your gift". (Matthew 5:23-24). We must follow this same example in dealing with the Father. Remember, "All

have sinned and fall short of the glory of God".
(Romans 3:23) When we realize that the ball is
always in our court, we take the pressure off of
ourselves. It's our chance to let it all out, clear our
consciousness of our faults and blatant disobedience
to God's will. It's a great feeling to get everything
out in the open. True healing takes place, when we
are honest, and come back to the Father with
humility.

It's unfortunate that the human ego will cause a
person to stand on a lie, as though it was the truth. We
must consummate the thought of truth, that not only
have we wronged people in our lives, but also we
have wrong God. Many times we try to look over
factors in our lives that have caused our backslidden
state. But the first thing we need to know about
resolution is that we need to admit that we messed up.

Determine the time period that you left the fathers house for the far country. Determine the events that led to your plummet. Consider the changes made in your life while in the far country.

In my personal resolution, I had somewhat of a flashback. I could actually visualize myself before the far country. I could visualize myself while in the far country. And I could visualize what it would be like once I returned from the far country. Out of the three, the visualization of what it would be like once I came back from the far country was the one that really supported my decision to come home. I mentally compared the differences of me being in his arms and out of his arms. That's when I was able to determine what I had to do, to get back into the father's arms. Now look in the mirror. Consider your mind, soul, and body. Some of you are remembering what it was like to have communion and fellowship with the father, and the misery of not having that union.

While others look in the mirror and think, I'm ok. Look deeper; remember what it was like to have joy in sorrow. Reminisce on the strength during struggle and how the father constantly provided all of your needs. Vice-versa to these considerations, are all the factors that led you to this very stage of being reconciled. Consider that very moment that you turned your back on God (the father). Sure for some of us it was a gradual process (turning from God). But for others it was following a single act of sin.

In either case try to remember how you felt, when you decide you wanted to take your portion of goods and live life to the fullest without a father to answer to. Visualize the different levels that you reached in life without fellowship with the father (God). When the pressures of this life presented themselves, they were unbearable. For many of us we had to hit rock bottom before we decided to resolve the matter. For some, rock bottom was hit more than once. I heard a joke about rock bottom that made the point that some have hit the bottom of the rock so hard, that they began to dig. Instead of laying there or digging, we must find solace in the loving arms of the Father.

Now that we have the idea of comparison, on being in the father's arms and out of the father's arms. Let's consider the terrible act of turning our backs on the father (God). Even though God is kind, loving, forgiving, and caring, we left the union. Leaving the union with the father, with no return could cause us not to reap the benefits of the kingdom. In (Luke 9:62, "Jesus says That none who puts his hand to the gospel plough and looks back is fit for the kingdom"). Notice Jesus didn't say he wouldn't make it into the kingdom, but leaves room for the backslider to pick up the plough once again or return to the father and make it into the kingdom. Where would we be if our father wasn't full of grace and mercy? After considering all things in our waywardness, let's get to the resolution part. How can we mend what we ourselves have broken? Bring together everything that we have plundered. Let's look back at the Prodigal Son, so we can mirror or mimic his actions. The initial step of the Prodigal Son was to arise (action verb) and go to his father. The prodigal had to get up from the very place where he was and make the steps in the direction of the father.

So for us to resolve our relationship with the father, we must get up from where we are.

We must get up from the wallowing, of whatever pigs pen we are in and go. It doesn't matter how far you've went or how long you've be wallowing, make haste, now is the time for you to arise and go to the father. Like the Prodigal Son, our resolve should be carried out quickly. Many of us have stood in the shadows of resolution before, but put off the action part to a more convenient time. I pose a question to you. "Why put off for tomorrow for what you can do today?" (Proverb) We should do like the Prodigal Son, arise and while getting up, he kept in his mind that he had to go back. So many times people get up and then don't follow through with the process, so they end up in the same shape and in some cases worse than they were.

The Prodigal Son made it his business to make it back to his father. Hungry, weary, weak, and tired; he went. He didn't get halfway there and fall on the ground begging for help; because of his condition rather he made his way back to the father. I remember a few times I made the initiative to go back to the father, but didn't follow through with the plan; I didn't make it all the way back. Instead of going straight back home, I made a few stops and the stops got me in trouble. Those stops caused me not to make it home. I let situations allow me to lose focus of the plan of resolution. That's the thing about reconciliation, on the way back home, you still have to pass through the same places that you, used to frequent. You still have to go by the night club, you still have to go by the strip club, you still have to go by the liquor store, and you'll still have to go by the sex shop. But when you have your mind made up, that you are sick and tired of being sick and tired, you can face whatever it was that got you down, with determination that you are going to make it to the father. Imagine the prodigal, having to pass by those folk that he had parlayed and partied with, but he kept on until he made it home.

I'm sure while the Prodigal Son was full of energy and motivation making his way back home, there were former friends and acquaintances who tried to block his way. The same ones whom he squandered his money on, they was his ambition and tried to hold him back. Keep in mind that satan doesn't want you to mend the relationship with the

Father (God), because that would destroy his relationship with you. He knows that just as sure as you make it back to the father, he will have lost you. But if you have truly considered all and are truly sick and tired of being sick and tired. You will make your way back home. If indeed we return home we will find our father full of mercy, compassion, and grace; willing to accept us. In the story of the Prodigal Son, we see a vivid picture of mercy, compassion, and grace; portrayed by the prodigals father.

Notice what the scripture says about the Prodigal Sons returning: (Luke 15:20"So he got up and went to his father. But while he was still a long way off, his father saw him and was filled with compassion for him; he ran to his son, threw his arms around him and kissed him"). The father no doubt anticipated his sons return. Even his eyes were full of mercy, for they quickly saw him and were extending forgiveness. Before the son could verbally express his repentance, the father expressed his mercy and grace. This paints a striking resemblance of God (our father). Even before we call he answers us, because he knows what is in our hearts. Even at this very moment while, your reading this very sentence. He knows the desire that you have to return home. His arms are outstretched, waiting for you to resolve the matter.

Like the Prodigal Son, we have to find the means to an end. What that means my friend is to take ownership of the act of turning back to the father. That's what the Prodigal Son did; he took ownership and figured out a means to the end of the repercussions of turning from the Father. Now, notice what the Prodigal Son included in his resolution next, out of everything that he did, this next step is what counts the most in reconciliation. The Prodigal Son repented (Luke 15:21"The son said to him, 'Father, I have sinned against heaven and against you. I am no longer worthy to be called your son'").

Notice this son didn't repent until after the Father had extended his forgiveness. It's inevitable that it is in God's plan to forgive us of our wrong doings. And as many times as we petition him for forgiveness, he will grant us his forgiveness. The prodigal son was assured of his forgiveness, but he was also amazed that his Father had received him with such mercy. I'm sure his heart was overwhelmingly in sync with his Fathers mercy and kindness. But along with the heart of thanksgiving, a genuine confession must follow.

I remember the day I came back to the Father. There I was walking down the sidewalk, hearing the voice of the Father. There I was walking down the sidewalk in broad daylight, feeling the loving kindness of the Father. The mercy of God overtook me, I begin to tremble and shake. Tears began to gush out of my eyes. I had never felt that way before. I accepted Christ at an early age, but this was intense, this was amazing. The feeling I felt was a feeling of acceptance, even in my present condition. The Father has accepted me back, he has granted me a pardon, this was my big chance to go back into the arms of God.

So I'm walking, trembling and shaking, crying, and feeling overwhelmed with joy. Then it hit me, I had to apologize, I had to make things right. I fell to my knees, yes in broad daylight, while walking down the sidewalk. I didn't care who was around or who saw me, all I knew was, I had to express to the Father just how I felt. There I was trembling and shaking, crying, feeling overwhelmed with joy, and knees bowed on the sidewalk. Like the prodigal son, I verbally expressed what I felt. I began to admit and apologize for things I thought I had forgotten. What an intense few minutes, which seemed to be hours. I was finally giving it all back to him, not hiding anything, not holding anything in, and just giving it all to him.

Repentance in its rawest form, omits nothing. True repentance will cause the oldest of trespasses and sins, to resurface. Many times, while in the far country, we tend to obstruct reconciliation by concealing our sins. If you truly want to be forgiving, you must first release yourself of all of your sins and trespasses. I can imagine the prodigal sons, time in the far country flashing before his eyes. Overwhelmed with this unexpected welcome by his father, this son summed all of his sins and trespasses into a brief statement "Father, I have sinned". I'm sure while speaking these short words; this son was gripped with some of the most horrible moments of his life. The flashbacks had to stir him, because he expressed his feelings of himself, by making the statement "I am no longer worthy to be thy son".

It's amazing that one could be so accepting and so forgiving, as to look beyond our faults and see our potential. I'm sure this father saw the dirty rags his son wore for clothing. I'm sure he saw his blistered and calloused feet. When he hugged his son his hair smelled and hardships of a pauper were apparent. But the father looked beyond all of his faults and saw his son. I'm forever grateful for the love, mercy, and grace of God, for without them, I wouldn't be here right now.

# Chapter 6
## The Power of Reconciliation

*"The part always has a tendency to reunite with its whole in order to escape from its imperfection."*
*-Leonardo da Vinci*

*"The number one problem in our world is alienation, rich versus poor, black versus white, labor versus management, conservative versus liberal, East versus West . . . But Christ came to bring about reconciliation and peace."*
*-Billy Graham*

In this chapter, I want to deal with The Power of Reconciliation and all follows. In observing the story of the prodigal son, we notice that after being reconciled, he was re-clothed and overwhelmed with rejoicing. This is the exciting part, because if you have made it this far in the process of Reconciliation, you're in for a treat. Let's take another look at this son's life from the moment he repented. While examining the prodigal's life, I admonish you to examine yours. Look into the mirror of the prodigal son and relate to him. This very moment of self-evaluation, can change your very life. Try it.

The prodigal came home full of fear and hope; fear of being rejected and hope of being accepted. His father was amazing better to him than his fears and better to him than his hopes, not only received but accepted with respect. He arrived back to his father's house dirty and in a pauper's clothes and his father not only clothed him but decorated him with the very best. The father commanded the servants to bring the very best for his son. I'm sure there were loads of old clothes, and I'm sure they would have been suffice for this son, but the father was precise, don't bring a coat, bring a robe. I love the emphasis placed on the robe. No doubt this robe was taken from the prodigal's closet, his personal robe. Before the son left he had on a similar robe, a robe that had been tailored just for him. Now after returning with rags, he is clothed with a familiar robe. A garment that felt just right.

Consider this, when a backslider returns to the Father, he is given a familiar robe to the one he wore before he left. This consideration hits home with me, the moment I repented and was reconciled to the Father; I immediately had the fire and desire I once had. That's the robe, the initiative to please God. A garment fit for a child of God. Even though the robe fit me, I felt uncomfortable, because I had just went from being in dirty rags, to wearing a robe of royalty. Like the prodigal I had some concerns about how others would perceive me. A dirty son, wearing a royal robe, surely would be perceived the wrong way. Allow me to encourage you; don't be concerned with people's faces, comments, or actions, this is your time to make come back home. Don't allow anyone's personal proclivities or opinions, detour you from being reconciled.

Imagine this son, coming home dirty, and not only his brother, but the servants; sneering, pointing, and whispering concerning him. I mirror the prodigal dealing with this as well. I remember when I came back to Christ. I had that fire and zeal of God, to do my first works. My focus was directly on the will of God. But then something happened, I came in contact with those brothers and sisters who had never left home. I was expecting the same love and acceptance that the Father had given, but I was in for a surprise. So many sneered, pointed, and whispered concerning me; here I am 3 years later and many times, I still get the same responses. That's why the story of the prodigal became so real to me; I began to relate to how he must have felt.

The prodigal son is back home, wearing his royal robe, and still others didn't want to identify him as royalty. What the prodigal's father does next expresses the Power of Reconciliation. After instructing the servants to put a royal robe on him, he then instructs them to bring the royal signet ring. The father no doubtedly noticed the nasty looks and heard the criticizing whispers. He wanted everyone that had never left the house to realize one thing. That this was his son, no matter what he had done, he was now back home and has been reconciled and restored to his rightful place.   Isn't it a great thing that God doesn't see us, the way others do?

The prodigal son returns home with rags, barefoot, and hungry.   His father looked beyond all of this, because his intentions were to give him everything he needed.  Even though this son had wasted a portion of his inheritance, the father intended on granting him another portion.   Wow, it's great to know that our Father doesn't hold our sins towards us, but only desires for us to be reconciled back to him.   Once being reconciled back to him, he acts as though we never left him.  We may have squandered a portion of our inheritance, but be assured if you repent, return, and be reconciled; he will give you another portion.

Like the prodigals father, ours is forgiving, loving, merciful, and full of grace.

This son returns home in rags, torn shoes, and ripped of every shred of decency that he had. Take a note of spirituality of the matter. Firstly, his raggedy close are replaced with a robe; which represents the righteousness of Christ (Isaiah 61:10 "I will greatly rejoice in the LORD, my soul shall be joyful in my God; for he hath clothed me with the garments of salvation, he hath covered me with the robe of righteousness, as a bridegroom decketh himself with ornaments, and as a bride adorneth herself with her jewels"). Secondly, the ring is symbiotic of the seal of the Holy Spirit, by which we are sealed to the day of redemption. The ring is a royal symbol; it's a constant reminder of the kindness of the Father.

Being adorned with this ring signifies royalty, which is our rightful place according to destiny (Ephesians 1:11-14 In him we were also chosen, having been predestined according to the plan of him who works out everything in conformity with the purpose of his will, in order that we, who were the first to put our hope in Christ, might be for the praise of his glory. And you also were included in Christ when you heard the message of truth, the gospel of your salvation. When you believed, you were marked in him with a seal, the promised Holy Spirit, who is a deposit guaranteeing our inheritance until the redemption of those who are God's possession—to the praise of his glory). Thirdly, the preparation of the gospel of peace is as shoes for our feet (Ephesians 6:15 and with your feet fitted with the readiness that comes from the gospel of peace).

# MIRROR OF THE PRODIGAL SON

This son couldn't have known what was in store for him at home. Broke, busted, and disgusted; but he made the effort to return. He returned hungry and the father not only, but threw a lavish feast for him. Upon returning to the Father, you will receive the best meal. Jesus Christ himself is the Bread of Life: his body is the meat, and his blood drink. By eating and drinking of Christ, you shall not only replenish yourself, but you shall receive life (John 6:53 "Jesus said to them, "I tell you the truth, unless you eat the flesh of the Son of Man and drink his blood, you have no life in you"). This son had the opportunity not only to be clothed, but to be fed, with a meal that he would never forget. What a joyous occasion when a son or daughter returns back into the loving arms of the Father.

I must admit that the best decision I have made was to return back to God. Through drug dealing, prison, addictions, bad relationships, mental anguish, and the hardships of life of sin; I've found that the safest place in the whole wide world, is in the arms of God.

Hopefully, by this point you understand dynamics of being reconciled to the Father. No matter when you left, how far you went, or how long you stayed. Gods arms are forever stretched wide, waiting on you, his prodigal son/daughter. He is waiting on you to make up your mind to receive The Power of Reconciliation. You can be a recipient of this power right where you are. No matter what Spiritual, Mental, or Physical condition; you are in. Please recited this prayer with a genuine heart and undergo The Power of Reconciliation.

Father, I'm so sorry for sinning against you. I know I have wronged you. Father, I plead with you according to your loving kindness and tender mercies. Please Father take me back, please accept me as I am. I am broken and need mending. I am torn and need repaired. I am tired and I need rest. I am hungry and I need to be fed. I am thirsty and I need a drink. Father, please mend me, please repair me, please give me rest, please feed me, and please give me drink. Father, I beg of you, please bring me back into harmony with your love. Lord, I thank you for reconciling me. Amen

*AKILI XZAVIER WILLIAMS*

# About the Author

Akili Xzavier Williams is the Founder and Lead Pastor of New Direction Bible Fellowship in Pompano Beach Florida. He is also the Sr. Pastor of Mt. Zion Outreach Ministry in Pompano Beach Florida. Akili Xzavier Williams is the President/Ceo of Inside Outside Transition Consults, Inc. He has a zeal for ministry and endeavors to bring mankind back to God. Akili's ministry is one that stems from firs hand knowledge and a personal relationship with Christ. Akili received the call to ministry at the early age of 9 years old. After backsliding at the of age 17 years old, Akili lived a riotous lifestyle. A lifestyle filled with sex, drugs, and rock-n-roll; so to speak. Now, reconciled back to God, Akili preaches and teaches the messages of Reconciliation.

## AKILI XZAVIER WILLIAMS

Akili's style and delivery of ministry challenges the non-believer and believer alike, to make a connection with God. This connection is one that Akili believes we all must make, if we are to maximize our God potential. Akili's theological approach is transparent, prophetic, practical, and personable. Dr. Akili X. Williams has earned degrees, certifications, and licenses in Information Technology, Christian Counseling, and Theology.

Akili travels teaching and preaching in conferences, revivals, and lectures. Dr. Akili X. Williams shares his drive and initiative with his wife Amy Romain-Williams. Akili and Amy reside in Florida with their two children Devin James and Akilah D'yana

To book Dr. Akili X. Williams for lectures, seminars, conferences, or any other events; use the following contacts:

http://www.wix.com/insideout1/mirrorofprodigalson

http://www.iotransitionconsults.org

http://www.ndbf.webs.com

axwilliams@iotransitionconsults.org

axwilliams1@yahoo.com

(754) 234-0918